I0840770

Writing Emergency

Ninety-Nine Ways to Fight Writer's Block

By Kate Danley

Copyright 2018

Kate Danley

Dedication

To the Acme

Introduction

It feels like staring into a hole. You search for inspiration and there is…

Nothing.

You're a writer, you tell yourself. You can do this!

You put your hand on your keyboard. You stare at the blank page before you.

And are greeted by the darkness.

All your hopes and dreams crash down around you as you find yourself…

Stuck.

Listen, nothing annoys me more than authors who say there is no such thing as writer's block. It's akin to Mozart wondering why everyone can't hear a full symphony in their head.

How very special for them that they have never experienced this hell.

I'm here to say that writer's block is real.

And if you've bought this book because you're stuck? That's awesome! You're normal. You're in the right place! This is the part of the writing gig that keeps people from ever finishing their Great American Novel. Writing is *hard*. So congrats on joining the ranks of almost every author in the world, and congrats on being brave enough to look for a solution.

My name is Kate Danley and I'm an author. I write full-time. I've sold over 750k books globally, a book of mine hit the USA Today bestseller list, I'm both traditionally published and self-published (they call it "hybrid" in the biz), won a bunch of awards, I have a film and television option for one of my series, I've written over thirty books and a metric crapton of plays.

And I get writer's block.

Listen, I'm a hack. I am not a literary darling. I do not have an MFA. I do not have the luxury of ruminating over thoughtful thoughts as a fat advance keeps the creditors at bay. I write or I don't eat. My ability to keep a roof over my head is solely reliant on my ability to churn out words as quickly as possible and get them into the market before the electric bill is due. I have to do four books a year minimum, and I gotta say that when you're facing those sorts of realities, you cannot afford to get writer's block.

But I do get writer's block.

And you know what that makes me?

An expert on how to get those creative wheels rolling again lickety-split! I can get the party started when my soul feels like a grumpy 13-year-old being urged by a dowdy chaperone to dance.

This book is not meant to be read in order. This is an "All Hands on Deck" emergency toolbox. It is Things-To-Try-When-It-Appears-All-Your-Talent-Has-Left-You-and-You'll-Never-Write-Again. I've kept things quick-n-easy so you don't have to wade through a lot of words to get to the tools you need. This is a Writer Emergency and no one has time for that! You've got ninety-nine tips and tricks to get you through this rough patch and, I promise, one of them will haul you out of your rut.

Flip open to a page.

Try the exercise.

If it doesn't work? Flip to another page and try that one.

I use language related to novels and plays, but trust the rules are all the same when it comes to getting yourself out of the suck. We are all one in this pit of despair.

* fist bump of solidarity *

Now let's get cracking! Into the fray! Yeehaw!

#1 - Believe You Can Do This

Everything you have accomplished in your life has started with a decision.

Decide you are going to write this thing.

Decide you are capable.

Decide that it may get rough, but you will tackle the challenges and not back down.

I know so many people who want to write but never choose to make it a priority.

Decide.

Right now.

#2 – Recognize This is Gonna Suck

I'm going to let you in on a little secret.

Writing is terrible.

There is not a single professional writer alive who has not, at some point, questioned their life choices.

But I'm going to ask you to trust in delayed gratification.

Because just as much as this writing sucks, oh… the feeling of having written.

It comes with a sense of profound satisfaction. There is a joy that makes you feel like you could leap over hills and dales. Putting down that final period in that final scene? Your heart will soar!

But you cannot experience that level of happiness and wholeness unless you finish your project. So buckle in. Lean into the harness. Accept the fact that this is gonna suck.

But hope is on the horizon. It will get better. It will be worth it.

I promise.

#3 – Romancing the Book

Make your writing time a celebration. Give yourself a hit of happiness. Your brain likes dopamine.

Light some candles. Put on cozy socks. Turn on music that relates to your story. Take yourself out on a cool adventure for research. What do you imagine big, fancy writers doing when they write? Do that.

Yes, writing is ultimately just the words you put down on the page.

But your whole life fuels those words.

If writing is a drudgery, your brain will rebel. It will sit like an angry two-year-old being told to put on their coat, even if there is a blizzard raging outside.

Writing is about play.

Writing is the ultimate game of "pretend" and you are inviting people to share in your imagination.

Enjoy the journey.

#4 – Organize Your Space

Now, this is a double-edged sword, because sometimes organizing space can become a person's favorite form of procrastination.

But it's hard to think creatively when there is a pile of laundry staring at you.

Spend a day getting your office really lovely. Make it a sacred space. You'll be channeling the muse here. Make it somewhere you want to be.

Replace the gross blue lightbulbs you bought on sale with light that makes you happy.

Get a comfortable chair.

Buy yourself a plant.

Hang a poster.

Whatever it takes, make it a place where you want to hang out and think awesome thoughts.

#5 – Use Your Voice Recorder

Isn't it funny how you always have the perfect idea when you're someplace where you can't write it down? I used to do standup comedy and some of my best jokes came while I was sitting in the car, raging at the drivers around me. And I can't tell you how many people I know with BRILLIANT stories who never get started because they never learned how to type.

No one says that you have to write things down for it to count.

Record it.

There are apps that will even transcribe the text for you.

Grab the inspiration wherever it happens. Don't let it slip away.

#6 – Write Like Exercise

You wouldn't get off the couch and expect to win gold at the Olympics.

Same with writing.

You gotta train up to it before a marathon session!

Writing involves deep, fractal thought. Right and left brains are firing shots at each other and demanding brilliance.

The nice thing is that scientists have found willpower and concentration can be improved with regular practice. All it takes is working out your mind like you would go to the gym.

So, day one? Expect to only be able to think hard for about fifteen minutes. Day two? You'll probably be able to concentrate for a couple of hours. And after that? You're off to the races!

The unfortunate part of this story is that if you skip a day or two, your concentration levels will fall back to the fifteen-minute mark.

So, just make a decision that every day, you're going to write for a minimum of fifteen minutes no matter what.

No matter what.

#7 – Timers Are Your New BFFs

The most difficult part of every project is getting started. It is a battle every day. There are so many delights out there in the world but… instead…

sigh…

You're sitting down to stare at the blank page…

Writing can lose its luster pretty fast.

The strange thing, though, is that once you actually get started? Nine times out of ten, it is a joy.

This is a little thing you may have heard of called *self-sabotage*. It is ridiculous the excuses we come up with to keep ourselves from doing the things we love.

But the best way to fight this implosion is to take the first step toward healthy behavior.

Get a timer.

I prefer an actual, dedicated, digital timer. It's too easy when you use your phone to get distracted by a text message or an alert from Facebook. If you *really* want to have fun, go get yourself an hourglass egg timer – one of those with the sand that flows through.

Now, set your timer for fifteen minutes (or flip your hourglass) and, for the next fifteen minutes, you are not allowed to do anything but write.

The laundry will call from the other room. You'll remember an email you forgot to answer. Your best friend's birthday. An important deadline.

All legit.

But everything can wait.

All this exercise asks is that you spend fifteen minutes doing nothing but writing. It's fifteen minutes. Anyone can do anything for fifteen minutes.

And at the end of fifteen minutes, if you're tapped out, get up and go do something awesome for the rest of the day guilt-free.

But more times than not, once you get into the groove, you'll find you want to continue.

So, set the time for another fifteen minutes and go!

Write like the wind!

#8 – Star Pupil

Everyone knows how to draw a star, right? Five straight lines? Good. If not, there are some YouTube videos to help you with that.

SO!   This exercise is for when things are BRUTAL. When you can't focus or get things done to save your soul.

We all have days like that.

We're going to give you some stars for A+ effort by having you draw them yourself.

Get a blank pad and writing instrument. Bonus points if you have a gold pen!

Open your work-in-progress.

Commit to doing nothing until you complete all five lines in your star.

Start a stopwatch.

Start writing.

When one minute passes, take a split second to draw the first line of your star. Immediately go back to writing.

When another minute passes, take another split second to draw another line of the star. Immediately go back to your work in progress.

The interruption to draw the line should not distract you. It is just a quickly jotted indication that you survived a minute of writing. And then another minute. And another.

A star has five lines and in five minutes you will have a star.

You wrote for five minutes. HIGH FIVE!

Maybe try for three stars?

That's fifteen minutes.

Maybe five stars?

Get those writing muscle back in condition and I promise soon you will have a galaxy.

#9 – Grab the Time When You Can

We all dream of long, lovely mornings at a 1920s Remington typewriter, staring out into the dewy morning fog as the words come trippingly off our fingertips.

Writing, even full time, is nothing like that.

You gotta catch what time you can.

Wake up half an hour early. Go to sleep a half hour late. Write during your lunch break. Write while waiting to pick up the kids at soccer. Too often I hear people say they just don't have time to write. Nine times out of ten, that's just a fancy form of procrastination. Nine times out of ten, said wannabe-writer is terrified they might be terrible or, worse, that they might be brilliant.

Time is not an excuse.

Shonda Rhimes, Jeff Bezos, Tina Faye, Elon Musk, Oprah… they all grew their careers with the same hours in the day as everyone else.

You start with the time you have – five minutes. Ten minutes. A half hour at a time.

It adds up.

#10 – Turn Off the Internet

The average human in America checks their smartphone 150 times a day. They watch five hours of television. They are on social media upwards of nine hours a day.

Any of these statistics making you squirm uncomfortably?

Listen, there is usually plenty of time in the day to write if you're willing to jettison the distractions.

Until your manuscript is done, remove the social media apps and games from your phone. I promise that lining up pieces of exploding candy does not get you closer to your goals.

Change your password to something impossible to remember and log out of Facebook and Twitter. If you start getting the delirium tremens, replace it with things that help your brain with vocabulary and word recall like crossword puzzles.

Unless you're writing political thrillers or activism pieces, cancel your newspaper subscription and stop listening to talk radio. If you're spending your think-time spinning on the world's challenges, you're not focusing on your own. I even had to stop watching home dec shows.

The science behind it is that we have these things called mirror neurons. They cause us to mimic (or mirror) the actions we see. It's how we learn. When you were a baby, if you saw someone smile, your face mimicked the muscles and you smiled. As you grew, you could watch someone do something, and you could repeat the action. These neurons also insert our imaginations into the situations so we feel as if *we're* doing it. Heart pounding when you watch sports? Mirror neurons. They're trying to get you to learn how to play football by making your body feel like you are in the game. I found watching home dec and construction shows caused my mirror neurons to fire up and I realized it felt like *I* was coming up with all the creative solutions, and when I sat down to write my book, all my creative juices were tapped out.

Ya gotta unplug.

And I'm not saying you have to do this forever!

But the online games, social and news media, and television shows (especially reality shows) use the same techniques the casinos use to keep you clicking and checking. It is in their best financial interest to keep you stressed and coming back for more. It is in their best financial interest to not give you a natural stopping point. They want you to lose track of time.

So, cold turkey it.

Trust that you'll hear the important stories about your friends and family and world, because they are impossible to escape. You are surrounded by people who are all participating fully in the social media drug and they will gasp desperately, "OMG! Did you hear about XYZ?" To which, you can say, "No! Tell me about it." And then have a lovely conversation.

But trust the world will spin just fine without you for the few months it will take to finish this book.

Can't unplug entirely? I get it! My entire business is pretty much dependent on online interactions.

But there are apps available which limit the time you're allowed online. I have a site blocker called StayFocusd/Freedom that locks me out of the internet at a set time each day and there's no way to turn it off. I also only get 90-minutes of time on social media and my other time suck websites and then I am blocked. I have a Chrome plug-in that replaces my entire Facebook newsfeed with an inspirational quote. There are programs out there. Can't afford the cost of an app? That's okay.

Physically unplug your router from your wall.

#11 – Limit Your Time

So often I hear people go, "Oh! If only I didn't have a day job! THEN I would be able to churn this book out!"

Trust me, it doesn't work that way.

We all need limits on our time, narrow windows with clear boundaries for how long we are going to focus. To say we're going to engage in deep thought for twelve hours is usually pretty unrealistic, and we'll end up doing none hours.

But to say we're going to engage in deep thought for two fifteen-minute sessions every hour, and continue that pace between the hours of 8:00 AM and 11:00 AM?

Break it down into the smaller, bite-sized bits.

Give yourself a start time and an end time.

Even better, make it a daily schedule. Your body will start to go, "Oh! It's 7 PM! It must be writing time!"

#12 – Accept if You're a Night Owl or a Morning Lark

Are you a morning lark or a night owl? Or both, but need an afternoon nap?

There are gurus who will tell you, "I get up at 3:00 AM and write 5,000 pages before breakfast!" and others who say, "I don't start getting creative until midnight and then I stay up until 4:00 AM churning out the words."

Free yourself from the guilt.

Both are right. For *them*.

But your job is to figure out what time works for YOU.

Figure out your natural rhythm, accept it, and schedule your writing time for your most productive hours.

Make it easy on yourself.

#13 – Buy a Journal

Get dressed. Head out to your local bookshop. Revel in the smell of new books, the sense that just by deciding to write, you are a part of this wonderful world.

Now, head over to the blank journal section. We're going to judge your book by its cover.

Pick out a journal that makes you go: "If I opened this cover, I would like to see my book inside."

Now, pick out a lovely pen. They usually have them by the wrap counter. Make sure it feels good in your hands.

Then buy them, go home, and write the story you want to find on your journal's pages. Carry your journal with you everywhere. Jot down notes, scene ideas, blurbs of dialog that pop into your head. Tuck in pictures you find, maybe tape in a map of the town where your story is going to take place.

This is your grimoire. Fill it with the magic of your story.

#14 – Inspiration Board

They say a picture is worth a thousand words, so if you are writing a 50,000 word novel that's… what… 50 pictures?

I kid!

Sort of.

So, the human brain likes to draw connections. When we look at two things, the mind automatically goes: "How are these related?"

We're going to use this to our advantage.

And we're going to kick it old skool.

What you're going to need is a bulletin board or a piece of poster board or just a section of your wall.

And now you're going to either go to your computer or grab a bunch of magazines and look for pictures that feel like they relate to your book. They might be pictures of the place your story is set in, the interiors of buildings, actors or oil paintings that look like your characters, or just things that create the feeling in you that you want to inspire in your reader.

Print those pictures up, cut them out, and hang them on your wall.

It's really important to put them where you will see them.

Because what will happen is that every time you walk into the room, your eye will fall on that collage. And every time your eye falls upon that collage, your subconscious brain will kick in with ideas on how those images relate to one another.

BOOM!

Suddenly your mind will start planting ideas.

Even better? When you get lost down the road of writing your project (and you will), all you have to do to get re-centered is to stand up, stare at your collage, and ground yourself in those images. They'll remind you who your characters are, where it is all taking place, and what you want to do.

#15 – Buy a Book Cover

I encourage you to pre-judge your book by a cover!

Buying a cover while you're writing your novel helps focus you on what you want the words inside to say.

There are book designers all over the internet. Some of them are cheap, some of them not so much, but many have these discounted products called "premade covers." The design is done, they just change the title and insert your author name. See if you can find a good one for your book, or get some stock photos and slap the title of your book on the front using a free design program like Canva.

And then hang your cover over your desk.

#16 – Ask Questions

Flummoxed?

Ask yourself a question about your project.

My favorite is: "What happens next?"

The human mind is meant to solve problems. If you don't give it puzzles, it will fret about world events or why your significant other can't eat with their mouth closed. The next time you're on the internet (AFTER you meet your daily writing goals), take a look at how the click-bait tries to lure you in. They give you an open-ended statement that makes you ask yourself a question.

"You won't believe what drivers in your area should never do."

Suddenly, your mind goes, "Wait. What shouldn't they do? Is there something I shouldn't do? What is this about?"

And you click because your mind needs the solution to the question.

Use this hardwiring to your advantage.

Give your mind a puzzle to work out about your work in progress, plus a little quiet time to think, and it'll chew on that question until it has a good answer for you.

It *likes* it.

#17 – Clear Your Mind

When you wake up in the morning, how long does it take for your mind to start spinning on all the stuff you need to do?

These thoughts will shape your whole day, and often will crowd out your creativity.

For five or ten minutes every morning (feel free to use a timer), just vomit out all of the garbage in your head onto the page. Write down everything your brain is spinning about as fast as you can. This is not a writing exercise. This is a process of clearing out your thoughts to make room for the things you actually *do* want think about: namely, your book.

#18 – Go for a Walk

There is research that shows repetitive physical motion frees your brain to engage in deep thought. If you're stuck, rather than flipping on your computer and scrolling through the endless narrative that everyone has their life together except you, go outside. Get some fresh air. Restock your body's supply of vitamin D. There is a big, bright, beautiful world filled with inspiration.

But before you go…

Identify a question about your story. If you're stumped, take my favorite: "What happens next?"

Then launch yourself out the door.

I highly recommend bringing some sort of a recorder with you because the ideas are going to start exploding like the kernels in a movie theater commercial popper.

As your feet wander, let your mind wander, too. Think about that question you had for yourself. Note the people you see and ask yourself if any of them belong in your story. Anything funny happen while you are walking along? Anything out of place? Anything taking you by surprise? How would you describe the smells around you? The sounds? The colors? The pace? You actually need these sensory experiences in your story to connect the reader to your writing, so mine that creative ore for all it's worth. Note how it feels in your body and try to think of ways to describe it in words.

I'm betting by the end of your journey, you'll end up in some exciting new places.

#19 – Listen to Some White Noise

Like repetitive motion, soft, white noise can also free your brain to think deep thoughts. Studies found the optimum level for creative output is around 70db, about the level of a café or water faucet. When you're in total silence, your ears are catching every disturbance, sending signals to your brain along the lines of, "What's that? I think it was a tiger. Do you think it was a tiger?   ARE WE ABOUT TO BE EATEN BY A TIGER?"

It can be a bit distracting.

But by providing a gentle hum of non-engaging noise, the ears relax. And when the ears relax, the brain can go off to solve the other problems on its plate.

Namely, your troublesome plot point.

There are a ton of online sounds. On YouTube, you'll find seven-hour loops of ocean waves and rainstorms. There are some apps for your phone, so if you're in a public place, you can hook in your earphones. I enjoy streaming the noise of coffee shops and restaurants from the comfort of my office chair. There's even some atmospheric scores created for role-playing games – sounds of a dungeon or a spaceport or an elfin forest. Maybe even some non-distracting music that fits the feel of your book.

Plug in and drift off.

#20 – Let Yourself Get Bored

The brain hates to get bored.

It will start looking for ways to amuse itself. And I'm here to say you can harness this and redirect it to your work-in-progress.

Set a timer for twenty minutes. Identify a question about your work-in-progress to ask yourself.

And now, for the next twenty minutes, you are not allowed to read anything, watch anything, listen to music, check your phone, talk to anyone, eat, smoke, drink, etc. Nothing.

Wait.

You can do one thing.

You can write, if you feel moved to do so.

Sit on the couch and bring a pad of paper and a pen with you.

It is SHOCKING how quickly the mind will come up with solutions to your book when you're bored.

And if you're on a really tight deadline and HAVE to get your project done, go cold-turkey for a full day. Or three-days. Or week.

When you take a look at the broad spectrum of global spiritual or religious paths, most of them encourage "vows of silence," solitary walkabouts, retreats, or cloistering one's self to achieve enlightenment.

Now, I'm not advocating sitting on a mountaintop for twenty years to figure out if your hero should escape a burning building by parachute or helicopter, but in the universal human experience, the people who specialize in higher thought processes seem to acknowledge there is profound power found in stillness.

So, you know, sit for a bit. Give it a think.

#21 – Clean something

Cleaning may or may not be an enjoyable experience for you, but it's probably not in your Top 10 Ways you'd like to spend a vacation.

What we're looking for here is a task that doesn't require a whole lot of brain power. Skip the laundry, because you have to think about folding and storage and do these pants make me feel fat? But that's just me.

Look for a task that is pretty monotonous. Scrubbing the tub. Vacuuming. Sweeping. Dusting. Mowing the lawn. Weeding. Watering the plants.

When faced with a boring, mildly unlikeable task, the brain creates ways to escape the current situation. And what better escape than into the world you're building in your imagination?

So, before you begin, ask yourself a question about your work-in-progress. It plants the seed of what you're going to think about.

And then polish those floors till they shine!

#22 – Read Books in Your Genre

90% of human thought is repeating things. The other 10% is input: seeing, reading, touching, hearing, smelling, experiencing. Treat that 10% as something precious. It will inspire the other 90% of what goes on in your conscious brain.

If you're spending all your time reading New York fashion magazines, you're not giving your mind the fodder it needs for your historical fiction piece about 13th century China.

So during this time that you're stumped, immerse yourself in your project's world. Read books in your genre. Read books that have the feel you're going for. Do some research.

Your brain will take all of this input, chew it up, recombine it, and create something beautiful from all

the pieces. Like a collage. A word collage. OF
YOUR IMAGINATION.

45

#23 – Watch Movies in Your Genre

Now, let's be clear this is "research" and not "escaping from writing." You get to do that escaping thing as a reward AFTER you finish your daily writing goals.

But for the sake of this example, let's pretend you're writing a murder mystery. Fire up some Agatha Christie on your television set, and bring a pad of paper and a pen.

You're about to take a masterclass in storytelling.

And you're going to want to take notes.

How did the writer structure the opening scene to keep the viewer from changing the channel? How do we meet the protagonist and other characters? What is the central conflict? When is new information introduced into the plot? What moments are suspenseful and how was the suspense created? What are the twists along the way? How do they do the big reveal?

Dissect the structure of the script and pay more attention to the "how" vs. the "what." By the time you're done, you'll have a notebook full of ways other writers have solved story problems.

I'm just betting one of the techniques might help you over your own hump.

#24 – Outline

For some people, outlining comes naturally. If this is you, keep doing what you're doing.

For others, outlining will make you wonder if there is a god and, if so, why does they hate you so much.

If you fall into the latter camp, this exercise is going to be pretty unpleasant. And, for the record, I'm a pantser (a.k.a. I figure out the plot as I go. I write by the seat of my pants.) But, if you're stuck, it is a way out.

You don't have to figure out your whole plot. You don't need to do a detailed five-page outline with an abstract like they tortured you with at school. No one is grading your outline. This is just a way of organizing your thoughts so you don't have to break your brain anymore.

Open up a document. Write a bulleted list of everything you've figured out so far in the order it appears in your book. Sometimes it is helpful for me to organize it chapter by chapter. Sometimes, it is just a list. If you don't know already, decide how you want your book to end (you can change this later!).

Now, look at the list of things you know. How can you get from the point where you don't know what happens to the point where you DO know what happens? Write down as many awesome solutions you can think of to connect those dots and see if any of them pique your interest.

Sometimes getting stuck is related to the infinite possibilities before you and freezing in the face of that many choices. Your brain can't hold that much info! So, winnow it down. Write down a one-sentence plot decision and allow your imagination to go down that path. See where it leads.

And, again, outlining is rough. You're basically writing a whole book in your head, but figuring this out over the course of a couple days via a bulleted list vs. spending weeks writing 20k words that you'll have to cut later can save you some heartache.

And again, this outline is just for you. You can throw it all out if you come up with a better solution later. You can change your mind. You can rewrite it or choose to ignore it. But by going through the exercise, you have a map. You know where you're going and when you get lost, you can consult it and go, "Oh, hey! Here I am! I took a wrong turn at this point, but can turn this car around and get back on track toward my destination."

#25 – Write the Dumb Scene

You know it is a dumb scene. You know that it has no place in your book. Aaaand yet… your brain won't let go of it.

So write it already! Words are cheap!

The steamy scene between the characters who you don't want to get together? The melodramatic dying scene of a character you aren't going to kill off?

Whatever it is, just write it down. Play. Clear it out from your head. And then copy-and-paste it into your "ideas" document and let it go.

#26 – Write the Worst

Sometimes we are so scared of getting it wrong, we freeze in our tracks. So, take ten minutes and stare that fear down.

Write the WORST version of your book as possible. I mean, the WORST.

The version you would never let anyone see.

Get it out of your system.

(And strangely, you'll find some gems in there.)

And as you go forward, remember you can always fix what you've written, but you cannot edit a blank page.

#27 – Kill the Darling

There is a point when my book has gone off the rails, and I know where it went wrong. But I look at my manuscript and cry to the gods, "But I don't waaaant to cut all those lovely words I spent aaaall this tiiime wriiitiing!"

Cut the words.

Kill the darling.

Fix that thing you don't want to fix because you know it is going to mean more work.

To soften the blow, open up a new document and cut-and-paste the stuff you're about to delete. There have been times I have been able to incorporate the thing I didn't want to cut back into my story. Bank it for later!

But clean up your manuscript.

Rip the band-aid off.

Be the hammer and bring it down.

#28 – Cut the Recaps

Something we do as writers, when we are lost, is that we have characters redescribe the scene that just happened. Unless you're Miss Marple about to reveal a critical detail to point the finger at the killer, recaps are just treading water. The reader was just there! They just read it! Don't make them read it again!

It comes down to making a decision. Any decision will do! Preferably, asking yourself what the coolest thing that could happen at this particular juncture is an excellent choice!

But if you're recapping, it means you've either forgotten what you just wrote (go back and read it) or you're scared of making a decision.

Make the decision.

#29 – Don't Be Afraid to Get Your Characters Into Trouble

No one *wants* trouble. For the most part, we want to get through life with as few emotional scars as possible, and we want the people we love to be happy and safe.

But as an author? This instinct to protect can murder your story.

As a teacher of mine once put it, if you were walking along in real life and saw a lion sitting in an open cage, you would probably try to get away from it.

But for a story? We want the character to interact with the lion: to get into the cage with the lion, to have tea with the lion, to get eaten by the lion. "And then I was chased by a lion!" makes for a much better tale than, "And then I called animal control and everything was fine."

Remember that your characters are imaginary and it is okay to hurt them.

Getting them into trouble advances your plot.

Do something terrible to them.

And then don't fix it.

Allow them to grapple with it. Allow there to be real fallout and consequences. The trouble should cause them to grow and view the world differently. Make sure it changes them. Keep the reader hooked with the question, "Oh no! Is this character I love going to be okay?"

And just when things look like they're *finally* going to be okay?

Do something terrible to them again.

#30 – Pick C, All of the Above

You're sitting there, frozen by two equally good options for your story.

Both are tantalizing.

Both are delicious.

You can't figure out which one to choose!

Guess what?

Choose them both!

Words are cheap! You can have as many as you want! Write both! I promise that about three pages in, one option will emerge the clear winner.

#31 – Deadlines

We are time guppies.

We will expand to fill whatever time we are given to complete a project.

Just think back to school when you had weeks to write a paper. Did you actually spend weeks on it, or did you cram it all into the end?

Deadlines are your friend.

I recommend getting a wall calendar for this exercise. It is too easy to ignore if the calendar is on your computer. You want the truth hitting you smack in the face every time you walk into the room.

Choose your writing deadline, the day you have to have your manuscript done, and write it down on the calendar.

And then start crossing off the days as they pass.

#32 – Admit to being Lazy

Listen. We've all been there. You know what needs to be changed. But the enormity of it all? The MOUNTAIN of work you have already done and the MOUNTAIN of work that awaits you if you actually do the thing that needs doing?

It would make anyone open up their internet browser to take a quiz on what flavor of Doritos best matches their personality.

I get it.

But…

You're going to have to do it.

The only way around this is through.

It is not going away.

But I promise that the amount of time you're procrastinating on *not* doing this thing is waaaay more than the time it is going to take to actually do it.

So…

Do the thing.

#33 – Track Your Progress

It is so easy to feel like we have spent a lot of time writing when we haven't. Or haven't spent any time writing when, in fact, we've been killing ourselves.

Data is your friend.

Write down how many words or pages you're writing each day. Track the days you write vs. the days you don't. Track what time of day it is when you naturally feel like sitting down with your manuscript.

As most health professionals will tell someone struggling with weight loss, the act of writing things down creates awareness. You naturally make adjustments when you have to be honest about what's really going on. It feels icky to have to write "Zero Words" on your spreadsheet. Sometimes, rather than doing that, you'll find yourself going, "Well… maybe I can spend the next fifteen minutes writing SOMETHING."

Get honest about what you're actually doing.

Write down the truth.

#34 – Word Count Goals

You know how you eat a whale? One bite at a time.

So, let's pick up that fork and start chewing!

We're about to embark on the journey of Achievable Daily Goals.

Yes, functional, healthy, achievable goals.

Don't look at me like that. It will be good for you! I promise!

Pick a deadline.

Decide how long your project has to be. (I prefer word counts, but it is totally cool to use pages. No one is the boss of you.)

Now divide your pages or words by the days until your deadline.

For example, novels are anything 40,000 words or more. So, if I have set my deadline a month from now, I take 40,000 words and divide it by 30 days. I have to write 1,334 words per day in order to finish in time.

That was a dense paragraph. Here it is in a way that is easier to understand.

Words ÷ Days = Words per Day

40,000 words ÷ 30 days = 1,334 words per day

1,334 is my daily word count goal.

(There are approximately 250 words on a double-spaced page, so 1,334 words are about five pages.)

And I actually take it a step farther, myself. I put a sticker or highlight the days on my paper wall calendar when I reach my daily goals. The flashes of color from across the room let me see visually if I'm on track to hit my deadline or not. Colorful calendar? I'm doing great! Boring calendar? Ooo… something is off. Plus, you get to use stickers and markers!

#35– Accountability Partners

The world is filled with writers struggling just as hard as you are right now. So get out there and find some kindred spirits! Real life, cyber friends, whatever. They all work!

(And don't know where to find people? Try searching for writers groups on Facebook or writing forums on the internet. Hang out, get to know people, and then ask if anyone would like to be your accountability partner.)

Once a week, send each other an email. Set your goals for the next seven days and 'fess up to each other if you met last week's goals or not. Sometimes when things are particularly rough, my accountability partners let me send them my word count EVERY. DAY.

You may feel silly or embarrassed looking for this sort of help, but you know what? You're probably going to be giving just as much as you're getting. We're all struggling. Everyone needs a circle of support! Do it for THEM.

#36 – Writing Dates

Once a week, grab some friends and go out on a date with your project.

Meet at a coffee shop, keep chat to a minimum, fire up your computers, and write. At the top of each half-hour or hour, ask each other about your progress.

Your friends will keep you honest.

There is something about peer pressure. It creates a focus hard to find in the comfort of your own home. Saying "I spent the past hour watching videos about cats rather than writing" doesn't fly. Allow yourself a little dose of healthy competition. Who can stay the most focused? Who can write the most words? Who crumbles like a cookie and says, "Let's call it a day"?

And if you don't have writer friends, check out Meetup or the NaNoWriMo message boards. There

are groups going on in cities across the nation and
many of them list their gatherings on those sites.

#37 – Take a Class

So, I'm betting if you knew how to fix this problem, you would have fixed it already. Nobody enjoys the feeling of failing.

But sometimes we don't know how.

Sometimes we need outside help.

Sometimes we need… *gulp* a class.

I know! Scary thoughts! But it is okay to say you don't know something, and it is even MORE okay to turn to someone and humbly ask for guidance.

There are online classes! There are classes at local schools! There are free classes at the library! Videos on YouTube! There are classes about grammar and classes about structure and classes about creativity! This is an amazing age where education is available at our fingertips.

And, I gotta say, if you can get to an in-person class, I highly recommend it. When people talk about success, there's the old phrase, "It's who you know." Classes introduce you to allies.

Don't be shy about reaching out. You're not supposed to know everything. Allow yourself to be teachable.

Seeking out knowledge is not a sign of weakness or failure.

Listen, if we're not growing, we're dying.

So get out there and live.

#38 – Write a List of Options for Ten Minutes

I learned this technique from a guy who learned it from one of the head writers of a big sketch show on TV. She had to come up with fresh, new ideas EVERY WEEK. EVERY WEEK! Millions of eyes on her work silently (and not so silently) judging her! That is some pressure.

And this is how she faced the demands of the job.

Set your timer for ten minutes.

Now write all the ideas you can come up with about whatever is stumping you. Story ideas, titles, plot points, whatever. No censoring. Nothing has to make sense. Just write everything down that pops into your head.

When the timer goes off, look at your list. Is there anything there that solves your problem?

If so, yay!

If not?

It was a whole ten minutes out of your life. Set the timer and do it again.

#39 – Don't Write Hungry

Speaking of sandwiches… I can always tell when an author is hungry because the characters are focused on what they're going to eat as opposed to the fire-breathing dragon approaching the village.

Eat. Otherwise, your hunger will show up in your manuscript like a bathroom dream.

There actually is another facet to this.

Remember Maslow's hierarchy of needs? It is hard to be creative when you are worried about food. And I say to you that if your stomach is growling, your body will direct your attention there rather than to the world on the page.

Mind you, this isn't a Free Pass to Binge Eat All the Crap. Crappy food will make you feel crappy and your writing will reflect how you're feeling. But go eat an apple. Fuel the machine.

#40 – Disco Nap

Our thoughts are a series of chemical reactions, which release electricity across the synapses in our brain. Scientists have found, though, that there are waste products from this process and they clog up our neuroreceptors, resulting in a feeling of sluggishness and inability to focus. How do we clean this mess?

We sleep.

Ideas are sorted and stored. Excess crap is cleared out. And we wake up feeling rested and restored.

If you're having a tough time focusing, lay down for a disco nap. Fifteen minutes, no more and no less (otherwise, you'll head into deeper sleep cycles and need two to four hours to get through them all or risk feeling off for the rest of the day.) After fifteen minutes, you'll hop out of bed ready to dance the night away.

Or write that troubling manuscript.

#41 – Cut Back the Caffeine

Scientists have found that being a *little* sleepy actually frees up creativity. Think about when you were out late with friends. The jokes? The laughter? The silliness? When the mind is just a little sleepy, it starts to play. Sadly, the caffeine in coffee and tea keep us sharp. It's a great tool when you need to study for a test or have a spreadsheet to reconcile.

Or a book that needs proofreading.

But for creativity?

It can hyper focus you and keep those stray, random thoughts from drifting in, and sometimes those stray, random thoughts are where genius lies.

#42 – Stay Hydrated

When was the last time you had a glass of water?

55% - 65% of our bodies are made up of good ol' H2O, and when we don't have enough, our metabolism starts to shut down.

And when our metabolism shuts down, it means all of our body processes are working at a lower capacity, and that includes our thoughts.

So keep sluggishness at bay and raise a glass of crystal-clear goodness!

#43 – Go Back

Where did your book go off the rails? I'm betting there was a moment where you may have decided to take the safe route. Go back to that point and make a different choice. Try getting your hero into bigger trouble.

Or maybe you swung the opposite direction. You've written you hero into a corner and there is, literally, no way to get them out of it.

Nobody has to know this.

Go back.

Try something different this time.

It's like a "Choose Your Own Adventure" except you're writing it.

#44 – Plumb the Depths of Your Plot Points

Take a look at all the plot points you have put into your manuscript. Have you followed through on all of them? Did you set something up and then forget to resolve it later? Are there unnecessary complications to the plot that are throwing you? Cut out the stuff that isn't working so you can see clearly where you want to go. Fully explore the information you have introduced. How did each plot point change your hero? Or not?

One of the biggest mistakes I see in early manuscripts that there is this great big build up to A Moment. Our heroes are charging forward. Bombs are exploding. Choppers are overhead. And they get there to that promised Moment? And the author doesn't know what to do.

So, nothing happens.

In a panic, the author creates ANOTHER Important Place The Characters Must Go that's miles away. Cue the helicopters.

There's nothing in that new location that is magically going to appear to solve your plot problem. You're the only person writing this book. You're going to have to make a decision. Whatever you think they're going to find *there?* Make it happen *here.*

Pay off the buildup.

Today is the day.

So often it feels like we need to throw more and more "things" at our plots to make them long enough to be books. But more often than not, you have a trove of buried treasure just beneath the surface, waiting for you to dig a little deeper.

#45 – Write the Ending

You probably wouldn't go on vacation without having the address to your final destination. You need it to figure out which direction you should go. Don't end up in Omaha when you want to be in Albuquerque.

If you've started at the beginning and are having trouble figuring out what comes next, write the end, and then go back and figure out how you get there.

#46 – Pick a Word, Any Word

Go over to your dictionary. Open it up. Pick two random words and see if you can incorporate them into your story.

Look around your room. First thing your eyes fall on. You must like it or it wouldn't have been right there.   Can it be something important to your character?

Step outside. What do you see? A tree? Everyone needs a tree! How can you work it into your next chapter?

Listen, you might not keep your character's ode to a paladin-shaped penholder (my penholder, which is shaped like a paladin, is sitting right in front of me right now), but the brain likes games.

It's like staring at the stars at night. If you look directly, you don't see some of them as clearly as you do in your peripheral vision.

When you focus on a random word, your peripheral creativity kicks in and starts to spot stuff, too.

With just the thought: incorporate a paladin-shaped penholder, the questions start rolling in. Is it just a penholder shaped like a knight? Is it a man who has been miniaturized and frozen as a statue? Is it a magical object? Do I use it as a murder weapon? Was it a gift from someone special? Can it be used to reveal the core need in my character's soul?

That took me all of twenty seconds to free flow on (free flow is where you just write down all of the thoughts that come into your head. No censoring.)

Still skeptical?

Sit down at your manuscript and incorporate the word "duck."

See what happens.

#47 – Invest in a Dictionary and Thesaurus

I know we live in a digital age, but sometimes there are benefits to kicking it old skool. Buy a paper dictionary and thesaurus, and use them the next time you are stretching for a word.

As you flip through the pages, your subconscious mind will pick up on things without you even realizing it. Planted in your brain like seeds, those words will start to grow and appear like magic as you're writing.

You might be looking up the word "rogue", but your eye passes the word "rose" on the way there. And suddenly, you'll come up with the idea that your roguish lord is a secret gardener who leaves roses on the pillows of all his lady loves. Or your roguish detective discovers a dead body beneath the rose bushes. Or rogue reminds you of rouge, and maybe your heroine has a penchant for pink makeup.

Your brain likes to create connections between unrelated things, and the dictionary is full of opportunities.

#48 – Get Out of the House

You know what's great about a coffee shop or library?

There's no laundry to fold.

There are no dishes to wash.

There are no windows to be cleaned.

There are none of the million little distractions that will try to call you away from your manuscript.

Did you know that for every interruption, it will take (on average) twenty minutes to get back to the task at hand?

If you're having trouble getting your project done, try getting out of the house. Remove yourself from all the things your procrastinating soul wants to tell you that you should be doing instead. Set a goal (word count, page count, it doesn't matter) and then don't allow yourself to leave the café until you achieve your goal. And then buy yourself a cookie in celebration!

#49 – Do Some Research

Sometimes it is hard to write about stuff because we don't actually know what we're writing about. If you are feeling a little iffy and like you're faking it more than you're making it, dive into the research.

Research is SO much fun! You get to make yourself an expert on anything you like! I spent eight weeks in an outdoor theater learning Shakespeare! I ran around Sherwood Forest! I took a ghost tour of a haunted boat!

Can't hop on a plane and take off to a location half-way around the globe? We have a wonderful world fueled by the internet. There are videos on YouTube of every topic imaginable.

Now, don't stay there forever. I know a lot of people who spend so much time on research, they never get around to actually writing their book.

You don't have to know EVERYTHING. Just enough to speak with some authority.

Don't be afraid to put things on hold while you go out there and chase down the information you need.

#50 – Are You at the Half-Way Point of Your Story?

Here we are at #50.

The dreaded halfway point of any manuscript.

"Dreaded?" you ask. "In ANY manuscript?"

You've introduced your characters. You've given them the Big Conflict. And now?

Only two hundred and fifty pages to figure out how you're going to get to your delicious ending.

Around the midway point, almost every author I know hits a wall. I call it the "mid-manuscript slog."

Thoughts include: This manuscript sucks. I'm a terrible writer. I should just throw this out the window and start fresh. I should set fire to my computer. What sort of starter fluid works best if I were to set fire to my computer?

It's all in your head.

Doubts in the middle of your manuscript are normal. I promise it isn't as bad as you think. It's just that you are halfway through the desert and ready for an oasis.

Buckle in and power through.

#51 – Character Date

Go someplace where your characters would go. Get to know their world a little more.

"But I'm writing a sci-fi space opera!" you cry.

There are creative ways to do this!

Let's see… sci-fi space opera… Is there an amusement park near you where you can experience the sensation of Zero-Gs? A jungle gym that looks like a geodesic dome? Desert landscape? A planetarium?

When I was writing *The Woodcutter*, a period fairytale based on the Brothers Grimm, I found a local pizza joint called Pinocchio's with carved beams and murals on the wall.

It doesn't have to be exact, but there's *something* in your town that ties into your book. If there wasn't, you wouldn't be writing it. Something planted that story in your head and is fueling your interest. A park. A monument. A store.

So go out and enjoy the heck out of it.

And whenever you're stuck, go back.

#52 – Cuppa

Like Pavlov's Dog, you can trick your mind into writing by giving it rituals. I have a specific mug for each book I write. When I sit down at my computer with that particular cup, I know it is time to work. I don't drink from it at any other time than writing time.

And when I have to switch quickly between multiple projects?

Change mugs, change your mind.

Deep, man.

So give yourself a touchstone of some sort. A song that you play before you write. A sweater you put on. A spray of perfume. Some sort of physical, sensory ritual.

Pretty soon, you'll be salivating to put down the words.

#53 – Dim the Lights

Again, one of those weird studies. It turns out that writing in lower light unleashes creativity. Perhaps it goes back to the time when we had to use the daylight hours to hunt and farm and mark off other survival tasks from our to-do list.

But the night? The night was made for storytelling around the fire.

So who knows. Evolution. Don't fight it.

Fire up the lava lamp. Get out the candles. Make it cozy.

#54 – Organize Your Characters

In theater and film, there's a thing called a makeup morgue where you keep track of the makeup design for each character. The vixen needs "Cherry Red – 01" lipstick, "Ben Nye" blue eyeshadow, and hair is loose and curly. The lead male gets beat up in the second act and needs a bruise on his left cheek. It helps the makeup artist keep organized and able to replicate the design night after night.

Do this for your novel.

It doesn't have to be big and fancy.

Just write down your characters as you introduce them. Write down their names, hair color, eye color, height, weight… basically any identifying characteristics. Attach some pictures of how you imagine your characters. Note any background information: Where did they go to high school?

What was their college major? Favorite food? Favorite song? What kind of car do they drive?

Figuring out some background (which you may or may not share with your reader) helps you to create more three-dimensional people on the page. If this seems like something helpful, do an internet search for "character analysis" worksheets. Actors use them all the time when they are stepping into a role. And you, as an author, get to play ALL the roles in your book.

I can't tell you how easy it is to get derailed from the flow when you're trying to remember what sized shoe your character wears. You tell yourself not to worry about it, that you'll look it up later, but secretly, you're sitting there going, "What size was her shoe?"

Write things down and keep it close by.

#55 – Cast Your Book

It can be so hard to keep characters straight. What do they sound like? What do they look like? One of the many things you have to think of as a writer is how one character sounds different than another character. Do they use slang or do they speak formally? Is everything a question or do they have all the answers? Do they whine or explode with declarations?

Added to all this, you have to remember what thcy sound like fifty-pages later.

I've found the best way to do this is to cast my books just like I would cast a movie. Preferably with actors who have distinct voices I can really hear in my head.

In the olden days, one might refer to these actors as your "muse." They are artists who inspire creativity in you.

Imagine your muses in the scene you're struggling with. What do they say to one another? What do they do? If they are rich and alive in your imagination, I find you almost don't even have to think about it. They unfold your story for you like a dream, and your job, then, is just to take dictation.

#56 – Time Jump

Sometimes you're in the middle of your manuscript, you are going hard and fast, and suddenly… there's a scene you just don't want to write. You know EXACTLY what is coming afterward, but the thought of tackling *that* scene is sending you into a spiral.

Skip over it.

I give you permission.

Now, do your future-self a favor and don't fall back on this toooo many times. You're going to have to write that battle/mushy/detailed-info-about-how-a-combustion-engine-works at some point.

But if it's stopping you in your tracks right now, go down a couple lines, make a note: [Insert dragon battle scene here.]

And move on.

#57 – Tropey

Sometimes you have to know the rules to break the rules.

Story genres tend to have tropes that an audience has come to expect.

For example, in a romantic comedy, two opposite people hate each other. Then, something happens where they discover they have more in common than they thought. But oh no! There's a misunderstanding or an unfortunate truth that is revealed! Their hearts are broken. But with some soul searching, they realize they are not complete without the other person and through forgiveness and acceptance and a change to their old ways, they get together and live happily ever after.

As goofy as it may seem, readers like tropes. There's a sense of order. The story went exactly as it should go. If your readers are expecting a romantic comedy, but your couple breaks up at the end, you're going to get some angry letters.

Do tropes feel a little stifling? There's actually freedom in the structure. You don't have to figure everything out. Tropes give you the tent poles to which you will attach your story.

And perhaps try thinking of tropes less as "clichés" and more like the kick line at Radio City Music Hall. How disappointed would people be if they got all excited to see the Rockettes, showed up, and the Rockettes were doing Martha Graham? Martha Graham's great! But when you're all geared up for a precision drill line and get interpretive dance, it's not what people signed up for.

And, as one author to another, it is okay to give readers what they want.

That said, it is also okay to break the rules, too! You're the author! Write what you want.

But if you're stuck, maybe spend a moment to look up the tropes of your genre and see if any of them can be useful.

#58 – Get Away From It All

I know… all of us are broke. But sometimes getting away from it all gives us the room and quiet we need for deep concentration. What might take three months to write squeezing in between soccer practices and dance classes can be tackled in a single weekend. I have a friend who books one of those cheap, last minute cruises to write – seven days with no internet, all meals prepared. She does nothing but sit in her cabin with her laptop.

Rent an AirBnB for a weekend.

Look up artist retreats. They're available across the country (and with enough planning, some of them are free.)

Or ask a friend who has a spare bedroom if you could sneak away to their place for a weekend or maybe swap houses.

#59 – Stop Comparing Your Insides to People's Outsides

Someone from high school has all you ever dreamed and you are a spectacular disaster. You practically live in the mud and eat worms. You look at your manuscript and hate it because it will *never* get you a life like So-and-So has.

Stop the pity party.

Your lack of success has nothing to do with them.

That person you envy? They have their own insecurities that keep them up at night. It's called the human condition. Trust me. If they're human, they've got the condition.

Jealousy and envy are tools of procrastination.

But they are also signposts for things that you want. And it is okay to acknowledge you have wants.

Shift the jealousy and envy to help you identify your goals. What has this person done that makes your heart yearn? Write it down. What things were necessary in order for them to achieve their success? This is your "To-Do" list. And before you say, "A rich uncle," did they really?

And, listen, sometimes the deck is stacked against you. According to a study called The Count, only 28.8% of all the plays being produced in America were written by women and only 15.1% by people of color. But we live in this amazing digital age where we don't have to wait to be anointed from on high. I had five years of rejections on my first book. Agents still won't look at me. My entire career exists only because I self-published.

If the gatekeepers are keeping you out, build your own castle.

And yes, there is a thing called luck, and yes, I know you want some.

But the strange thing about luck is that it is entirely dependent on the person being prepared to receive it when it knocks on their door. Are you ready? If a publisher calls you up tomorrow with a million-dollar advance, do you have a brilliant, completed manuscript to hand over? Have you edited it? Do you have options available if they say, "You're great, but this book is not the right fit. Do you have something else?"

Do the work.

The miracles happen at the rate necessary for you not to screw them up when they arrive.

#60 – Write a Mission Statement

Oh man, back when I used to haunt cubicle land, someone bringing up the corporate mission statement would elicit an eye roll so hard, I'd sprain my optic nerve.

But guess what?

Mission statements can actually be useful tools.

If you're frozen because you don't know whether this is a good thing to write or should you write this other thing, pause for a moment.

Write up a mission statement.

Don't worry if it seems goofy. Admit to that embarrassing goal you hold in your heart.

Just write down what values are important to you, what you want to accomplish, and how you want people to perceive you.

Here's an old mission statement of mine:

To write imaginative, fun worlds that are unique to my point of view. To write artistically satisfying projects that excite me and I am proud of. To write projects that create opportunities for myself in theatre. To achieve financial stability and freedom from debt. To increase my output and decrease my time on social media. To achieve a balance with my mind, heart, and body. To produce commercial theatre I am proud of, to write plays I am proud of, and to be a professional actress people invite back to work with again and again.

Your mission is not an end all, be all. A lot has changed for me since I wrote that statement above. And you should rewrite your mission statement at least once a year. But as you make decisions about projects to put on your plate, run them by your mission statement. Does this project aid you in achieving your goals or does it veer you off your path?

Things become really clear.

#61 – Go to a Book Reading

Go to a book reading by a fancy, superstar author. Glean all the wisdom and experience they have to share.

Go to a local book reading by an author who seems just a few steps ahead of you.

Politely ask them questions about the thing you're struggling with. Get inspired by the idea that this future is possible for you.

Sometimes it is easy to feel defeated by the thought that you are going to work and work and work and work and it will add up to nothing. The only authors we hear about are the ones with the fancy agents and million dollar contracts.

But finishing your book is possible. Having a career as an author is possible. Learn from the people who have what you want.

There's an old saying that if you keep doing what you're doing, you'll keep getting what you're getting.

Pretty depressing.

But if you flip it…

If you do the work and follow the recipe for success this person you admire has done, you may be able to accomplish what they've accomplished.

Or perhaps, a bit more simply: Learn from the best.

They've lit the way for you, it is up to you to follow in their footsteps.

#62 – Keep a Notepad by Your Bed

Have you ever been in bed and come up with the PERFECT idea? Maybe you said to yourself, as you closed your eyes and snuggled in, "I'll remember it in the morning."

And by morning you've forgotten?

Or have you ever had a dream and woken up going, "WOW! That would make such a cool story!"

But by the time you've gotten up and brewed your coffee and found a pen, the idea has disappeared?

It happens.

Keep a blank notebook by your bed.

If you get that perfect idea, roll over and write it down.

You don't even need to turn on the lights! Grab the notebook and pen, keep your head on the pillow, and write in the dark. Sure, it might be a little more difficult to decipher in the morning, but it will be there.

Once you start this practice, you'll be shocked by all the cool solutions your subconscious mind is trying to get to you in half-sleep. Some of mankind's greatest inventions started as dreams, and it is only because their inventors had the wherewithal to pay attention.

Listen to the whispers of genius.

It's all there, right in your noggin'.

#63 – Cool Factor

Once, I was SO stuck. I could barely go on, I was SO BORED with my manuscript.

So, I sat down and looked at my plot.

I had my characters traveling to a mountain where they smelted some iron to make a sword.

Smelted iron.

SMELTED IRON???

At what point is smelting iron the most interesting, dynamic choice for moving a plot forward?! It's melting a bunch of rocks and hitting them with a hammer!

I cut all of it out, gave them a magical sword, and threw them into battle.

If you're stuck, take a look at your manuscript and see if anything is happening. Are they wandering aimlessly?   Are they telling the other characters they'll reveal the vital, important secret 'later' but first they should all sit down and eat a sandwich? Are you stuck in a scene with the dramatic tension of buying paper towels?

Cut all that stuff out!

We don't need all the details.

Today is the day!

Make it happen NOW!

Make every plot point in your book something that delights you!

Ask yourself, "What is the coolest thing that could possibly happen?"

Then write that!

Save the sandwiches for your book signing party.

#64 – Brain Exercises

I was once in a car accident and knocked several points off my IQ. I was determined to get my brain back and in as good a working order as I possibly could.

So, I started doing research on people with Alzheimer's and dementia. What exercises did doctors recommend for keeping sharp?

Crosswords, Sudoku, memory games… I worked on memorizing some standup and eventually graduated to Shakespeare. And I'm proud to report that twenty-seven of the books I've written came after that bump on the head. Seems something worked.

The information on brain health changes constantly. As I type this, there are probably twenty new findings. So, look up Alzheimer's and dementia research, and see if there are things you can

incorporate to keep your mind firing on all cylinders.
A healthier brain helps every facet of your life.

#65 – Health

I am not a doctor –BUT– our brains require some form of healthy fat in order to operate at peak performance. Fish oil, Omega-3s, olive oil, avocados. The mind also needs energy to work (the brain burns 20% of your daily calories) and sometimes that means you'll find yourself craving sweets and junk food when you write.

Opt for fruits and vegetables. Make sure you are getting your vitamins. It's hard to feel peppy and alert when you've got an iron deficiency or are crashing after binge eating a bag of cookies.

We are nothing but meat machines careening around this world, and when you feed a machine poor quality fuel, it quits working. Your brain is a part of your body, and if your tummy is upset because you fed it a block of cheese and two pizzas, your mind is going to be thinking about that instead of your masterwork.

Make sure your nutritional needs are being met. Take care of your body. It's the only one you get.

Feed your head.

#66 – Exercise

It used to be believed that the brain could not generate new brain cells. Once you killed them, they were done. But recently scientists found that it IS possible to generate new brain cells – and that's through exercise.

But not just any exercise!

You have to be having fun while you're doing it.

So dance, fencing, swimming… whatever gives you a sense of joy. That feeling of euphoria is a sign that you're doing it right.

Fun AND a healthier body AND a brain that works better?

Seems like a win-win-win to me.

#67 – Sign Up for Improv or Theater Classes

As daunting as they might be, acting is an art form based on storytelling and words. It will increase your vocabulary and understanding of story structure – either through having to memorize the words of others or having to make up the words on the spot by yourself.

If you go for the improv, personally, I would recommend long-form. Short-form is more focused on games and laughs. But long-form is about being able to sustain a story for twenty to forty-five minutes. Sometimes it is comedic, sometimes it is tragic. You have to learn how to introduce characters, how to get specific, make decisions, how to create conflict and story arcs, and how to resolve things at the end. It is all stuff you need to know as a writer, but it will be learned through all of your senses – mouth, ears, eyes, body. And I don't know about you, but in science class? It was SO much easier to understand what we were learning in the book after we did an experiment in the lab.

And learning acting from a scripted piece? You'll discover how to construct characters, how interactions can change the meaning of the words, subtext, rhythms, and pacing. You'll begin memorizing the text of some of the greatest writers in history. Their brilliance will be stored in your head!

Improv and theater are an opportunity for a hands-on education in writing.

And there's something about interacting with other creative minds on a weekly basis, too. You'll start seeing the world a little more expansively, a little more fearlessly.

#68 – Reunited and It Feels So Good

There is some book in your life that made you fall in love with writing. Some book that made you go, "I want to do THAT!"

Go back to that book.

Remember why you fell in love with reading and writing.

Reconnect with that part of your soul.

Allow yourself to be inspired by your hero.

#69 – Move the Rut

Habits tend to keep us in stasis. We do the deal and get the same result.

But if you're stuck, sometimes a little change is in order.

Rearrange your room.

Jolt your mind out of its stupor. Make it cope with things not being how they usually are.

Put your desk on a different wall. Change the colors around you. Hang up a poster. See the world just a little differently each day.

#70 – Don't Talk to Anyone About What You're Doing

When you talk to others about your ideas, it releases the steam from the pressure cooker. Allow things to build inside until you MUST share them on the page or you'll explode.

Because if you start talking to people, they will, with only the best intentions, start to give you suggestions. There's an old saying that you can judge how good an idea is by how many people want to rewrite it.

They will cause you to doubt.

And this can throw you off track.

This is YOUR idea. There is no one else on this planet who is capable of telling this story besides you.

So protect this precious gift.

#71 – Talk to Someone

Conversely, bounce some ideas off people.

Hearing someone talk about their unwritten plot is about as interesting as listening to someone talk about a dream, so use this option sparingly.

But if you have creative friends you trust, ask them if they have a solution for whatever is stumping you.

It will go over better if you have actually put words down on paper to show you're serious. It's like when you put out a great, big email at work and start to get questions. I don't know about you, but I feel a lot more kindly toward the people who have read it and need some clarification vs. the people who haven't read it, they just want me to save them some time.

Just a word to the wise: Take what works and leave what doesn't, and never argue the validity of their solutions. "Thank you" is a perfect response to a terrible idea and, yes, sometimes people will give you terrible ideas. But sometimes those terrible ideas can knock the gears back into place and allow you to see the right solution.

Take the note and smile.

But if you do have someone who listens and helps you out, make sure your next conversation begins with a grateful, "Thanks so much for that insight! It really helped!"

#72 – Write Something Else

Ever been at work and all you can think about is what you're going to do when you get home? And then you get home, and all you can think about is what you need to do when you get back to work?

This human tendency is a tool you can harness for your own work-in-progress.

If you're writing something, but your mind can't stop thinking about a different idea, pause for a moment and go spend twenty minutes working on that other project. It is totally okay to work on more than one book at a time. If some idea is burning its way into your soul, by gum, sit down and hack it out! Switch between two projects! Switch between three! No one is the boss of you!

While you're over working on Book #2, your brain will often start working out the issues on Book #1.

The brain is funny like that.

Play along.

#73 – Write the Scene from the Opposite Point of View

Sometimes we get so wrapped up in the hero's journey, we forget we have a cast of supporting characters to help us on the page. If you're writing about the protagonist, try writing a scene from the antagonist's point of view (or vice versa.) You probably won't want to use it in your actual book, but think of this as a way to gain insight into whether your other major characters are well rounded or if they are being underutilized.

And if writing it out is too daunting, just trying reading your story and imagine how the chapter would be different if another character in the room was the star. Sometimes seeing your world from a different angle will let you see which gears need a little extra tightening.

#74 – Bad Reviews

There is nothing as soul crushing as sharing a bit of your soul with the world and getting a bad review.

You can tell yourself as much as you like that it doesn't matter… but it does.

Stop pretending it doesn't hurt.

Stifling your feelings cuts you off from the emotions you need to be an artist.

We must have thin skin that regenerates quickly.

Mourn it. Feel lousy for a night. Eat a cookie. Complain to trusted friends over the injustice of it all.

My favorite technique is to read the review out loud in the most mocking, mouth-breathing, whiniest voice I can muster.

And then come back tomorrow and double-down.

#75 – Acknowledge the Stuff Going on in Your Life

Listen. I know we all want to be machines and power through every day, but take just a moment to do a reality check.

Has someone you loved died recently? Did you lose a job? Are you having a fight? Health scare? Feeling financially insecure? Wondering where rent is coming from?

It's really, really hard to operate creatively when you're worried about these things. It can be done, but it is important to acknowledge the outside stressors.

You must name your monster in order to vanquish your monster.

There's this idea in psychology called Maslow's Hierarchy of Needs. It's a pyramid of things that we have to have covered before our brain will give us the space to think about bigger ideas. At the base of the pyramid, the things we *have* to feel secure about if we hope to survive include: food, water, shelter, and rest. Once you get those covered, you start to think about: Am I in a safe neighborhood? Am I going to get robbed on my way home? Once you're stable enough to have survival and safety covered, you can start to think about relationship needs and esteem needs, and waaay up at the tippy-top of the pyramid is "Creativity." What Maslow suggests is that we have to feel pretty okay with where we're at before our brain is able to stop worrying and let us think about other stuff.

It is okay to take some time out to handle whatever situation you've got going on. It is okay to take a day or a week or a month to stabilize.

But if you're in a spot where you can't stop, you have to write this thing or else face dire consequences, read on.

#76 – Breathe

Take a minute to breathe. If this sounds goofy, it seriously is only going to be a minute. Inhale on a slow out of five, hold your breath for a two count, exhale on a five count. Repeat for a minute.

#77 – Meditate

There are some apps called *Calm* and *Headspace,* there are all sorts of great meditation resources on YouTube, books at the library, free meditation gatherings in local parks, churches and spiritual centers... It doesn't matter what you choose to do, but if your head is going crazy and not letting you write, take ten minutes every morning to meditate.

It's not about making the thing you're worried about go away, it's about allowing you to detach long enough from it to get your stuff done.

Don't worry.

If it doesn't work, it's been a whole ten minutes out of your day.

#78 – Compartmentalize

Your world is going nuts. Your head won't stop spinning. You can barely think straight.

Sometimes our brain keeps chewing on things because it wants to make sure we remember to solve the problem, even if it is a problem we can't solve.

So, we're going to physically put your worries away for a little while.

You'll need some paper, a pen, and a box.

Write down everything you are worried about on individual slips of paper. EVERYTHING. It doesn't matter how big or little.

Write it down, fold up the paper, put it in the box, and say to yourself, "I've written it down. I don't need to remember this anymore."

And once you've gotten to the bottom of your worry list, put the box away and say, "This box has all my problems. They'll be here for me when I'm

done."

#79 – Share Your Icky Emotions

We are so often taught that negative emotions are *Bad*. We must hide them from the world and pretend things are fine.

But if you're in a dark place, maybe consider that this is something you can channel into your work vs. allow to block your work.

If you're feeling sad, write about the saddest thing in the world. No one understands despair better than you do right now.

If you're feeling depressed, write about the awfulness.

If your heart is broken, write a different ending to your story.

If you're feeling any of these things, chances are there are some readers out there in the world who are feeling them, too.

So, share yourself with them.

How many times have you turned to a book for escape and understanding?

You don't have to have answers, but sometimes it can be a gift to let other people know they are not alone.

And if you are in the mire, sharing your slog can help someone else get through theirs.

Don't be afraid to share your struggles.

Use this tough time to help others.

#80 – Hate Write

Listen, we all have that person we love to hate. The person we're only friends with on Facebook because we want to revel in every mishap that befalls them. 'Fess up! You know there's one person who makes you a poster child for *schadenfreude.*

Now, I'm betting there is a book or a movie that you *HATED*. You watched or read it and went, "How could the writer have blown it so bad!" You revel in watching it tank at the box office and silently judge people if they say they like it.

Now is your chance to write… erm… right that wrong.

Write the story the way you thought it should have gone. Rewrite the ending you hated so much.

Maybe even take a look at a moment in your life that you wish had unfolded differently and write the "alternate universe" version. Did someone do you wrong? Perhaps they are the perfect inspiration for your villain.

If you feel so strongly about something that you're holding a grudge, milk that grudge for all it is worth and turn it into some art.

#81 – Honor Your Heart

Write something you love.

I know! I know.

Sometimes you're on contract. Sometimes you have to write stuff that holds no interest to you. I've been there.

But make sure to balance out the suck with joy. There is no delight quite like sneaking in a secret assignation with a creative project you adore between the brain drain of what you're being forced to do.

Make space for your heart.

Take ten minutes to write something that makes you smile.

#82 – Haiku

5-7-5

That's the structure of a haiku poem.

Five syllables in the first line, seven syllables in the next line, and then a final five syllables. They don't need to rhyme.

Writing a haiku causes you to think about meaning. You must be specific. And because it is such a short poem structure, you are rewarded with a finished piece in a matter of minutes.

Haiku reminds you

That you *do* know how to write.

Each word has power.

#83 – Rewards

Listen, we're all just big kids, and the reward system is not just for kindergarten. Get a bowl of small, loose candy. We'll use M&Ms for this example. Every time you hit 100 words? Have a piece. If you pull 2,000 words in a day, that's a whole 20 M&Ms (a serving is 210 pieces, so you're in safe territory.)

If you're watching your figure, other options include: getting a sticker book and putting in a sticker every 100 words; dropping a pretty marble into a glass jar; getting some of those counting toys (small, plastic, brightly colored toys. When I was a kid, they were shaped like teddy bears) and lining them up on a shelf; put a quarter in a jar and at the end of the week, you can spend your loose change however you want.

Whatever little reward you like! Just set a small, achievable goal and every time you hit that small, achievable goal, give yourself a small hit of happiness. Train your brain to think of writing as fun.

#84 – Get Your Head in the Game

Self-talk is a powerful tool. It is so powerful, religions and spiritual orders around the globe use mantras, prayers, and repeated sounds to get an idea out of the head and incorporated into the entire body.

So, let's get this idea that you can do this on your lips, in your ears, and resonating in your bones.

Stand with your legs spread, fists on your waist and chest held proudly, or go look in the mirror.

(Shut up, you are gorgeous.)

Say out loud, "I am a great writer." (Or whatever it is that you need some help believing about yourself.)

Say it loud and proud.

Repeat it over and over until you stop feeling dumb and you start to believe it.

And then do it again tomorrow.

#85 – Stop Writing in the Middle of a

This technique may or may not work for you. But when you're done writing for the day, stop typing in the middle of your last sentence.

It'll kind of sit there, itching like a mosquito bite. Your brain will think about it. And the next day, you'll come back and be ready to leap right in.

Give it a shot and see if it works for—

#86 – Protect Your Time

Every time you are interrupted, it takes twenty minutes to get back on task. Every day you procrastinate on a task, it takes (on average) two weeks more to get the project done.

Protect your time.

Turn off your phone. Turn off your notifications. Turn off your incoming email. Tell your kids to go watch TV for a half-hour. Whatever it takes.

You don't get any more than twenty-four a day.

We all have obligations and you certainly need to make sure you're fulfilling your responsibilities.

But it is okay to claim time for writing like you would claim time for going to work or whathaveyou.

You don't have to destroy relationships for this writing thing, but if you've said you're writing for fifteen minutes, by gum, fight for those fifteen minutes.

#87 – Love Notes to Your Future Self

Sometimes you'll be in the middle of an epic scene, things are torquing along, you get an idea for something earlier or later in the book, you go to fit it in… and you lose the thread your muse so generously had handed you.

Keep a notebook or an open document close at hand. Take notes on that brilliant idea, but stay connected with where you are. See that first bit through to the end before heading off to the new and shiny.

#88 – Beware Grass Grows Greener Syndrome

You're in the middle of a book. It is getting rough. And suddenly, you get this BRILLIANT idea for a book you need to write RIGHT NOW. So, you abandon your work, and start work on the new book… and you hit the halfway-through-mark… and things are getting rough… and then you get this BRILLIANT idea for ANOTHER book.

What we have here is a classic case of "The Grass Grows Greener" syndrome.

The unfortunate truth is that whatever book you're writing, the only person at the keyboard is you.

–OR-

As the old saying goes, where ever you go there you are.

Each book you write will teach you a different skill set. But if you never push past this rough part, you'll never figure out how to overcome it. You've only figured out how to quit when the going got rough. And in every future project, once you reach this particular problem point, you'll stop because you're stumped.

Growing sometimes hurts.

Growing sometimes will break your brain.

But if you can accept this truth, push through it, and complete the project, you'll know how to face it in the future and overcome it.

Stick with your book. Nothing else calling your name is going to be any easier than what you're doing now.

#89 – Whad'ya So Scared of, Baby?

Fear and creativity can't exist in the same plane. It's a survival thing. If you've gone into a cave and attracted the interest of a hungry bear, Mother Nature wanted to make sure your full attention is on getting away from the bear and not going, "Wow! With a few twinkle lights, I could really spruce up this joint!"

But here in our modern world, sometimes we get afraid of things that are not life-threatening. Sometimes we are scared of looking silly or of people making fun of us or of revealing too much and, with our heart on display, being rejected for it.

This is an imaginary fear. This is a procrastinary fear. It keeps you nice and safe in your hole.

The cool thing with fear is that once you name it, it tends to disappear.

So, look at your blank page. What are you scared of? Did you have a wicked step-father who told you that your writing was dumb? A pretty teacher at school who told you that you were stupid? Are you about to write about something terrible that happened to you and you just don't want to? Has failure been dogging you and you just can't put yourself out there anymore? That this is going to be a lot of work and you'd rather be watching television?

Name it.

Like all the fairytales told us, once you learn something's true name, you hold the power.

Name it. Stare it square in the eye. Wield your power.

And write anyway.

#90 – Inspiration Everywhere

If an athlete was getting ready for a game, and you heard them say, "I can't do this…," you would probably assume things weren't going to turn out so well.

Believe in yourself!

As if it never occurred to you, right?

Like breakfast, our morning thoughts are some of the most important of the day. We carry them around for the rest of our waking hours.

So, get your day started right!

Go online and do a search for "Inspirational Quotes." Print them out. Tape them on your bathroom mirror. Read them as you brush your teeth in the morning.

Take five minutes before you start writing to listen to some music that gets your heart thumping. Eye of the tiger it, yo.

Jump up and down. Get some oxygen to your brain.

If inspiration isn't coming to you, go out and hunt it down for yourself.

#91 – Refuel

You would never expect a car to run without gas.

When was the last time you refilled your creative well?

Went to an art gallery? Saw a play? Enjoyed a concert? Sat on the beach and watched the sunset?

Once a week, refuel your soul. Whatever it is that makes you feel alive, honor that part of you.

#92 – Instinct

There are things we know.

There are things we don't know.

Creativity lies in the things we don't know we know.

If you have been trying to control the creative process, relax and release. Stop leaving invisible claw marks in your art.

Trust you know how to get out of this block. It may just take you a little while to figure it out.

#93 – Swing Time

A study has found that swinging on a playground swing is helpful with banishing creative blocks. Your sensory input is united with your motor functions in a controlled, repetitive movement. The gentle rocking of the inner ear is soothing. The fun gives you a hit of endorphins. Ten minutes is all it takes to see the benefits.

#94 – Nobody's Perfect

Have you rewritten the same chapter twelve times? Is it keeping you from writing the rest of your book?

Don't let perfect be the enemy of good.

Your book will never be done. You will always find something to fix. And sadly, you can over edit a piece and squash out all the magic.

If you find yourself making lateral edits – meaning, you are switching one word for another, moving a line up and then back – you're probably done.

Move on.

Write the next chapter.

#95 – Save Editing for Editing

When we approach our manuscripts with an editing eye, we kill the creative instinct for play. We're trying to "get it right" rather than allowing our imaginations to wander.

Now, I do some editing as I go. Like getting into a spat, I usually don't think of the perfect thing to say until two paragraphs later.

But if you're stuck and you're finding that you're making a lot of edits, stop. Finish your first draft. Allow your chapters to sit in a messy, unkempt state. Comb out your snarled story later.

That's what second drafts are for.

#96 – Eavesdrop

When a stranger walks into a room, do you look up? Do you put down your phone? Do you introduce yourself? Do you ask this person about themselves and try to figure out what makes them tick? Are you even interested in finding out what they're about?

If you want to write about the human experience, you must study humans in all of their beautiful, damaged glory.

Inspiration is all around you!

People watch. Listen in on the restaurant booth next to you. Write conversations down. File crazy happenstances away for future use. Ask people questions and find out their truth. You'll find it really is stranger than fiction.

Embrace a spirit of curiosity.

#97 – Write Out of Spite

Piggybacking on #97 and naming your fears, we have two choices in life. In Zen philosophy, there is an idea that if you get knocked down seven times, get up eight.

So, hey, some jerk has hit you squarely with a roundhouse of suck.

Get up.

Write out of spite.

Write to show them that you may be down, but you are far from out. Ring that fight bell yourself with your bare-knuckle fist and start swinging. Show them that you are so much more than their narrow little worldview can possibly understand. Prove them wrong. Go write that book that's going to sell a hundred million books. Think about how you will laugh as you do the backstroke through your swimming pool of royalty money like Scrooge McDuck while they weep sad tears. Make them so sorry they ever underestimated you.

You are brilliant.

So, prove it.

Get cracking on your book and make it awesome.

#98 – Beta Read

Sometimes two heads are better than one. If you've formed a support network of writers you trust, reach out and ask if anyone would be interested in swapping manuscripts.

I don't know why it is, but it is SO much easier to spot issues in someone else's project than our own.

Give them your manuscript and get theirs. (And it can be a couple of chapters. It can be a whole manuscript. Whatever you need help with.)

Read it.

Give them supportive, constructive feedback on how to make things awesome while still preserving their unique voice and story. I bet reading an unpolished work with a critical eye will make you think of things you need to work on in your story

(unfortunate truth: we usually spot things because we're struggling with them ourselves.)

And then... *gulp*... get your manuscript back. Brace yourself and take it slow. The first time you get notes, it'll feel like someone called your baby ugly. I give you permission to take what works and ignore what doesn't.

But some of the best bits in many of my books are the result of my trusted reading circle helping me to see the light.

#99 – Quit.

That's right.

I said it.

Quit.

Ooo… does the idea horrify you? Thrill you? Are you sighing with relief?

All reactions are totally valid.

But if you've been bashing your head against a brick wall and getting nowhere, I hereby give you permission to quit.

Quit! Flip the table! (Don't actually flip the table. You have some very nice things.) Tell your muse to take this manuscript and shove it where the computer screen don't shine! Storm out in a blaze of glory!

Then revel in the delicious feeling of quitting! Do all those things that sitting with your stupid manuscript didn't allow you to do! The manuscript was getting you DOWN. But now? No one's the boss of you! You do what you want! Watch the TV with no pants on! Eat all the pizza straight out of the fridge! Give life the ol' middle finger and tell it you're not playing anymore!

And then…

Tomorrow.

Come back.

And try again.

I'll be right here for you.

So, there you have it. Ninety-nine ways to fight writer's block. Do you need one more?

Sign up for my newsletter to get #100!
BookHip.com/BZHLFS

And if this helped you at all? Tell a friend. Leave a review. We all need a helping hand.

About the Author

Kate Danley is an award-winning playwright and novelist. She spent over five weeks on the USA TODAY bestseller list and has sold over half-a-million books globally. She has been honored with the Garcia Award for Best Fiction Book of the Year (*The Woodcutter*), McDougall Previews Award for Best Fantasy Book of the Year (*Queen Mab*), and her series *Maggie MacKay: Magical Tracker* has been optioned for film and television development.

Her first full-length script, the 1930s screwball comedy *Building Madness*, won the 2016 Panowski Playwriting Award. Her second full-length script, *Bureaucrazy*, was a semi-finalist in the 2017 O'Neill National Playwrights Conference and 2018 Moss Hart & Kitty Carlisle New Play Initiative. Her one-act *Power* was the overall winner of the Renegade

Theatre Festival. Her short *Kings of the World* was honored as the 3rd place audience favorite in the 10x10x10 Festival, tallied from over 400 ballots. Her plays have been performed in Los Angeles, New York, Chicago, Ottawa (Canada), Bath (UK), Grande Prairie (Canada), Seattle, Houston, Baltimore, and Anchorage, among others.

She graduated from Towson University with a BS in Theatre Summa cum Laude and was named a Maryland Distinguished Scholar in the Arts. She trained at RADA London, The Groundlings, Folger Shakespeare, Theatricum Botanicum, and Acme Comedy Theater. She also attended the CTI Intensive and subsequent workshops in commercial producing, the Kenyan Playwrights Conference, and the Arvon at the Hurst writing program in radio drama. She performed her original stand-up at such clubs as The Comedy Store and The Icehouse. She belonged to the main company and wrote sketch for a weekly show in Hollywood. She won the Breckenridge Festival of Film Screenplay Competition for her feature script *Fairy Blood*. Her film shorts *The Playhouse, Dog*

Days, Sock Zombie, SuperPout, and *Sports Scents* can be seen in festivals and on the internet.

www.katedanley.com

Books by Kate Danley

Visit http://www.katedanley.com for the full list!

The Woodcutter
Queen Mab
Olde Robin Hood

Twilight Shifters
The Dark of Twilight
Moon Rise
Light of Dawn

O'Hare House Mysteries
A Spirited Manor
Spirit of Denial
Distilled Spirits
In High Spirits

Maggie MacKay: Magical Tracker
Maggie for Hire
Maggie Get Your Gun
Maggie on the Bounty
M&K Tracking
The M-Team
Maggie Goes to Hollywood
Maggie Reloaded
Maggie Goes Medieval
Eine Kleine Nacht Maggie
Of Mice and MacKays

The Ghost and Ms. MacKay
Red, White, and Maggie

My Maggie Valentine

Miss Spell's Hotel

Queen Joanna
Galatea & Pygmalion
Dead Man: Reborn
The Spirit of Krampus

Write Till You Drop
Writing Emergency: 99 Trick for Busting
Through Writer's Block

Books by Agatha Ball

Paige Comber Mysteries
The Secret of Seaside
Murder's a Beach
Mystery Comes in Waves

Grey Skye Adventures
Skye's the Limit

www.ingramcontent.com/pod-product-compliance
Lightning Source LLC
Chambersburg PA
CBHW061759250726
48657CB00001B/202